The Good Island

Story by

Hawkeye S. Wilson

Illustrations by

Jeremie Lederman

$$v_{\text{esc}} = \sqrt{\frac{2GM}{R}}$$

Escape Velocity
Publishing

Phoenix, Arizona

$$v_{esc} = \sqrt{\frac{2\,G\,M}{R}}$$

Escape Velocity
Publishing

This book is a work of fiction. Any references to historical events, real people, or real places are used fictitiously. Other names, characters, places, and events are products of the author's imagination, and any resemblance to actual events or places or persons, living or dead, is entirely coincidental.

Rev 1.0- February 2014

Published in the United States by

Escape Velocity Publishing

www.evPublishing.com

Library of Congress Control Number: 2014902054

ISBN-13: 978-0615939759

ISBN-10: 0615939759

Contents

Chapter 1

Escape to the Forest

Ulysses darted between the tree limbs and leaves, flying in and out effortlessly. The hummingbird sang to himself while spinning his body. The pond was getting closer as he propelled himself forward.

"He's arrived, he's arrived!" Ulysses chirped excitedly. The hummingbird stopped and hovered over the loon that was floating in the water.

"But is he ready?" Barry asked, sensing the excited look on the hummingbird's face. "He is at the right age but will he venture to discover us? Will he answer the call?"

"I… I think so, I think so," Ulysses answered, darting closer to the loon. "He'll be ready! I have a good mind that he will find us!"

"We will see," Barry replied quietly, drifting further out into the water. "The real question is if he will answer the call."

*   *   *

Aaron rolled down the car window to inhale the scent of the pine trees as his dad drove him to their cabin. The Dailey family cabin was down a gravel road and hidden within the forest. The trees covered and shaded so much of it that Aaron often thought the simple shelter it provided was just a temporary relief from the greater excitement that lay within the forest.

Every year, the family would begin and end their summers at the cabin and every year the forest beckoned Aaron to its sanctuary. His first trek was just a few feet in, the sun still lighting his path. Another year, he ventured far enough in to discover wild mushrooms and red berries. Now seven, Aaron felt he would be able overcome his fears and go to its heart.

The car came to a stop and everyone exhaled in relief to reach their destination. The doors swung open and the family stepped out to stretch cramped arms and legs. The family removed their belongings and brought them inside. Aaron lugged his bag to his room and swung it up on the bed. He unpacked, putting the clothing that didn't go in the closet into the dresser drawers. After a small dinner, he fell into bed, exhausted after the long trip.

The next morning he pulled on an old pair of jeans, threw on a frayed baseball hat and found a flashlight with working batteries. He knew the forest was full of wonder but included its share of annoyances like buzzing mosquitoes, sharp sticks and dreaded poison ivy.

Aaron slipped out the back door and made his way to the forest. The sun began to rise and shed its light on the thick carpet of grass. It was easy to enter the forest because the trees were thin on its edge. No discernible path existed but he would make his own. He pushed aside branches only to watch them stubbornly swing back in place after passing by. He tiptoed through the crumbling decayed wood with a wary foot as if he didn't want to awaken anything from its slumber.

There were cobwebs across some of the trees which glistened with dew in the morning sun. Sometimes Aaron could avoid them, other times he found himself picking the sticky web off his face. The ground was soft and unmatted. He stepped further into the forest until he heard a loon's wail echo through the morning air.

That sounded close, Aaron thought, but it was difficult to pinpoint from where it came. If he followed its general direction, he might find the loon. The wail pierced the air again, a screaming pitch that started low before switching to a higher octave. Aaron occasionally heard the sound erupt into high and low octaves.

The forest bed soon became difficult to navigate, with large deteriorating tree trunks submerged into soft dirt. Aaron balanced on them, holding out his arms to keep his footing. The morning dew had not completely dried so the bark was slippery, causing him to lose his footing a few times.

He continued to make his way toward the loon's wail and hit a patch of dew that caused him to slip and stumble. He tripped and fell down, throwing the flashlight forward instinctively to use his hands to catch himself. His baseball cap slipped forward and covered his eyes.

Aaron stood up and took a moment to brush himself off. His knees were muddy and he brushed them as clean as he could. The flashlight was lying a few feet in front and as he walked forward, he was startled to find himself on the shore of a pond in the middle of the forest. It was surrounded by tall green grass with sunken logs poking out of the water. In the middle of the pond he saw an island that appeared to be in pristine condition. Aaron walked closer to the shore and spotted some stones. *Why not skip a few*, he thought?

Chapter 2

Birds of a Feather

"Why do you skip stones?" the loon asked.

Aaron stood on the shore of the pond with a stack of stones about his feet. He bent over to pick up another, held it close to his face and examined it for a smooth surface.

"I want to see how many times I can skip one," he replied. Gentle waves lapped at the pond's shore and the sky was blue except for a few wispy white clouds. The morning sun shined brightly and reflected on the pale blue water.

"That seems like a funny thing to do," said the loon. He swam over to where the boy was standing and watched him with keen interest. His body bobbed up and down in the gentle waves. "But then again, I've never thrown stones before."

After skipping a few more, a look of satisfaction settled over Aaron's face and he sat down on the small swath of sandy shore nestled in the green marsh grass. The water held a mesh of brown algae that danced underneath, darkening the pond's floor. Vibrant lily pads covered areas of the pond and some were blooming yellow flowers with red tinged petals. A breeze came and went, swaying the tall pond grass. Leaning back on his hands, he peered closer at the loon.

Instead of having the usual coloring of the black loons Aaron had seen in the past, this one was yellow, almost golden. The loon appeared formal and elegant, with a yellow head and beak and a uniform speckle of white throughout his body of feathers. It floated up and down in the water, undeterred by the pond's gentle ripples.

"I'm Aaron. Were you the one calling out last night and this morning?" he asked.

"Of course and I was hoping you would answer my call," the loon chortled. "My name is Barry."

"Has this pond always been here?" Aaron asked looking surprised. "I've never been this far out in the forest before."

"As long as I can remember," Barry chuckled warmly. "Yes, the water is all I need and is the source of so much life."

"I like it, especially that island out there," Aaron said, pointing to the middle of the pond. "Have you ever been there?"

"The Good Island?" Barry answered. "Sure I've been there. Why do you ask?"

Barry suddenly looked down into the water, his attention focused on something moving. With a quick flip, he plunged below the surface. Aaron stood up to get a better look and saw Barry swimming close to the pond's floor. Barry soon emerged and shook the extra water from his golden feathers.

"Why did you do that?" Aaron asked.

"Not everything is on the surface," Barry explained, his attention still diverted to below the water. "It's sometimes necessary to dive for what you need."

"Any good stones down there?"

"Never thought of looking before but- wait a minute," Barry said quickly before plunging below the water again. He reappeared, the water rippling outwards from his body. "Yes! I found them for you. On the bottom, you will find plenty of stones."

"That doesn't do me any good," Aaron said with a sigh. "I'm up here and you're in the water."

"Well," Barry harrumphed. "If you don't get wet, you can't get what you want."

Aaron paused and stared at the iridescent golden loon. He crouched, took off his shoes and rolled up his pant legs. He began to wade into the water, his feet slipping on the moss covered rocks.

"Why do you skip stones?" Barry asked, watching Aaron step slowly from rock to rock.

"I like to see how far they can go," Aaron replied. He squinted to look below the surface. Any move he made caused ripples, impairing his vision. He struggled to stay still, his toes gripping the rocks below. "I've even skipped one six times in a row!"

"Is that a lot?" Barry asked. "I just thought once you threw it that it would keep going. Like this. Watch!"

Barry dove quickly under the water again, resurfacing close to where he was before.

"Did you notice the ripples from where I was and where I am now?" Barry asked. "Did you see how the ripples overlapped each other and you can't tell where either one started?"

"So you're saying," Aaron began slowly, "... the waves become one because they're really just part of the water?"

"Yes," Barry replied. "Think of it as part of the whole."

"One in all, all in one," Aaron said quietly to himself.

"Did you see me when I was underwater?" Barry asked.

"No."

"But you knew I was there, right?"

"Yes."

"And I would come back?"

"Sure."

"Even though you skip a stone, how do you know it stops causing ripples?" Barry asked. "It's not because you cannot see them anymore?"

"That's a funny way to see it but then again...," Aaron said while struggling to keep his footing and get out of the pond, without dropping his stones. He had plunged his hand into the water and grabbed what he could. "You live in the water."

Barry smiled, his body bobbing up and down on the pond's gentle ripples.

7

Suddenly Ulysses stopped in mid-air and then flitted to where Barry was floating. His wings beat the air rapidly, while his tiny feet dangled beneath his green body. His wings beat orange while green feathers lined his back with a black head and tail.

"Ulysses, we have company," Barry said, his body lifting momentarily off the water with his golden wings extended and flapping. "Aaron was asking about Good Island. You've been there, right?"

"Sure have, sure have," Ulysses chirped almost as quickly as his wings beat the air. "Not many flowers, but keep in mind that there's a great view to see. To see."

"See what?" Aaron inquired.

"Different, different for everyone, but, but," Ulysses flew to a branch over Aaron's head and perched on it to take a rest. "You can see, you can see... better. Yes! You can see better! I remember!"

Ulysses noticed a flower and quickly flew to inspect it for nectar. The flower was ripe and he darted his beak in and out to lap up the treat. He then flew back to the branch over Aaron's head and the sun brightened the green feathers on his back.

"What brings you here?" Ulysses asked. "Here, here. Now, now."

"He's here now and he's our guest," Barry answered, shooing Ulysses' comment. "We are happy to have you!"

"Yes, yes, happy to have you, happy to have you," Ulysses chirped. He saw another flower and flew over to it, poking his head back in and out to lap its nectar. He zipped back, flew upside down and then hovered a few feet in front of Aaron. "What are you doing today, doing today?"

"I was skipping stones," Aaron said while lifting his arm up and flipping his wrist sideways. "Watch."

"What a funny thing to do, to do." Ulysses laughed. "I've never thought of doing that, doing that."

"That's how we learn though," Barry replied. "Just because we haven't done it doesn't mean it can't be done."

"You are so right, so right," Ulysses gulped. "So wise, so wise you are, Barry."

"Ha!" Barry snorted. "Even the wise never stop learning. It is better to be humble if accused of wisdom. True wisdom knows how little we know."

"Wisdom is more than memory too, memory too," Ulysses laughed. "I can remember every flower I have visited and when it will be full of nectar again but memory ain't wisdom. A mind can drown in memorization alone."

"So I can learn from you?" Aaron asked Barry.

"No, I cannot teach you anything," Barry answered. "I can only help you find it within yourself. I cannot teach anybody anything. I can only make them think."

The day had gone by quickly and the sun was beginning to lower itself in the sky. An evening breeze chilled the air. Aaron looked around the pond and watched the light dim in the forest. He watched a monarch butterfly flutter between the marsh grass.

"I have to go back now but I'll be back tomorrow," Aaron told Barry and Ulysses. "Will you be here?"

"Of course," Barry said happily. "This is our home and you are always welcome."

"Always welcome, always welcome," Ulysses repeated.

"Well, goodbye for now," Aaron said as he stood to his feet. He gave the pond another quick glance over his shoulder before disappearing into the forest.

"Will we see him again, again?" Ulysses squeaked.

"Yes, I am certain of that," Barry replied.

The stars began to poke through the canvas of the evening sky and their brilliance enhanced with the descent of the sun. It tossed off an orange hue that colored the clouds. Barry stared at the forest where Aaron walked into, lost in thought.

Chapter 3

The Shell Game of Reason

The next day Aaron returned to the pond's sandy shore. He walked with more confidence and saw his footprints still defined from the day before.

Aaron looked across the water to see where Barry was. He held his hand to his forehead to screen the glaring morning sun, and spotted the golden body reflected on the water, like a beacon. Aaron began walking around the shore to where Barry was bobbing up and down in the water.

When he reached him, Aaron found Barry talking to a turtle perched on a partly submerged log. The turtle's shell had lines across it, like panels, and his feet and neck were speckled with green and white. A light crust of dried mud stuck on the edges of his shell.

"Good morning, Aaron!" Barry said excitedly. "We were just talking about you. Meet Rex."

"Really?" Aaron responded. "Nice to meet you..."

"Were you the one skipping stones?" Rex snapped. "Why would you upset Nature's balance?"

"Now Rex," Barry intervened. "Where are your manners? Remember that the pond is big enough to handle a few more stones."

"I just can't see the Reason behind disturbing a perfectly good pond," Rex said to Barry, ignoring Aaron. "Where is the lesson in that?"

"A few ripples aren't going to upset anything," Barry responded quickly. "It will always return to its natural state. It's a big pond. Remember, we are part of Nature and life is good when you are in harmony with Nature."

"What are you guys doing, doing?" Ulysses said as he zipped over to them. "Good, good morning. What did I miss, miss?"

"I was trying to tell Rex that I was the one..," Aaron began.

"Good ol' Rex, always grumpy before breakfast," Barry interrupted. The group chuckled while Rex maintained a solemn, withdrawn look on his face. "Yes, it is always a good morning."

"I don't see what's so funny," Rex grumbled. "I can't see the Reason. No Reason at all."

Some at the pond, Barry explained, rely on Reason alone to see the pond. Everything that occurs, rain or shine, is seen and judged through the application of Reason. It was like a shade pulled over his eyes and Rex could not see the pond without it. He remained steadfastly loyal to Reason, as if it served him best.

"But he's upsetting the pond's beauty," Rex complained.

"Everything has beauty," Barry responded. "But not everyone sees it."

"Have you ever been to Good Island?" Aaron was a bit startled by Rex but persisted. "I'd like to go over there."

"Good Island!" Rex exclaimed. "Why would I go there? Everything I need is here or in the water. What difference does a little patch of land make? No Reason to go. No, none at all."

"Oh, well I thought I would ask," Aaron said, his eyes shifting to the water. A small gust of wind would cause the surface to ripple momentarily before it returned to a flat, reflecting sheet.

"Change and then change back," Barry said, reading the look on Aaron's face. "Just like soup, it needs to be stirred once in a while."

"Hmm, that's a good way to put it," Aaron said while sitting on a rock. "How is the water today?"

"Perfect," Barry replied, straightening a couple of golden feathers. "It is as it should be which is always perfect for me.

"You could almost say that there is a flow to it," Barry continued.

"A flow, a flow," Ulysses chirped.

Aaron sat down in the sand and began using his hands to shovel a pile together. The sand was still wet from the morning dew and felt cool in his

12

hands. It was easier to mold and soon he had enough piled together to begin shaping it. He used his palms to pat it down while his fingers carved out details. It was a crude castle but he looked at it with approval.

He stood up and clapped his hands to get rid of the excess grains. He looked towards the sun and was thinking about how the use of Reason prevented Rex from ever visiting Good Island but it didn't stop Barry and Ulysses. The use of Reason applied in some cases but not in others and differed in value between everyone. Reason, it appeared, depended on whatever turtle was under the shell.

"If we are all part of a Whole and that is our true natural state," Aaron said to no one in particular, "wouldn't Reason keep us from our true Nature?"

Rex's sour face changed to astonishment. Barry and Ulysses just smiled on silently.

Chapter 4

A Creature of Habit

"What are you guys talking about?"

A salamander crawled out of the marsh grass onto the log Rex was sitting on and stopped next to him. He had a long tail and his body was speckled with yellow and black marks. He had four toes on each foot and his mouth stretched broadly across his face. His tongue would occasionally shoot out like an arrow and disappear as quickly as it appeared.

"Hello Henry!" Ulysses excitedly said. "What brings you to the pond today, the pond today?"

"It's always been my Habit," Henry replied, looking over at Aaron. "I'm just not always on this side. I heard racket and decided to ramble over. Who's this?"

"A guest, a special guest," Barry began. "Aaron, this is Henry."

"Wow, I've never seen a salamander before," Aaron answered.

"Well, don't make it a Habit," Henry replied while looking for a bug to snack on. "I come and go as I please."

"That's true," Rex said. "He certainly does."

"So what's new, Henry," Ulysses chirped. "Any plans for the day?"

"Just the usual, nothing new," Henry replied, his tongue shooting out. "Nothing changes. My Habits are set so why change the routine?"

"Good ole' Henry, never changing," Barry chuckled. Aaron watched him as he dove under the water before returning to the surface.

"Hold on," Henry enthusiastically cried.

With a quick start, Henry ran towards Rex and launched himself into the air off Rex's shell.

"Hey!" Rex grumbled.

Henry landed in the water and swallowed as many water bugs as possible. He paddled back towards the shore, pulled himself up onto the log and sat next to Rex with a look of satisfaction.

"If it works, don't break it," Henry said. "My Habits are set in stone so why budge? Dependable, reliable, undeniable."

Aaron looked at Henry again and thought about how determined and loyal he was to his Habits. They defined his actions and made his thoughts rigid and stale. Henry was so occupied with maintaining his routine it seemed to extinguish his true Nature. Habits, Aaron thought, made you hollow and deaf to what you truly could be and your real purpose. They turned you into a creature.

"By chance, have you ever been to Good Island?" Aaron asked.

"Why go when everything I need is here?" Henry replied sharply. "Nope, no need to go."

By this time, Ulysses had flown to search for more flowers. Aaron saw him in the distance, zipping from one place to the other. He laughed to himself thinking how fast the hummingbird flew, hardly ever standing still. Just like fleeting thoughts.

"What are you going to do today?" Henry asked, pointing his body toward Aaron's direction. "Skip more stones? Disturb the peace some more?"

"No, I want to wander around the pond's shore," Aaron meekly replied. "This still is a new place for me."

"I'll be your escort," Barry gurgled. He had just returned from another dive. "You should meet some of my other friends. Where's Ulysses?"

"Right here, here," Ulysses squeaked. "Whew, the flowers are blooming today!"

"Don't you ever worry about running out of them?" Aaron asked.

"No, no I've never thought of that before," Ulysses answered. "Never had to worry about not enough flowers. For sure, for sure."

"The pond has always provided what we need," Barry explained. "There is no need to want more. It has always provided. It is in perfect balance."

Chapter 5

The Waddling Dogma Dilemma

"Well, c'mon Aaron," Barry said. "Watch your step and let's see if we can find Dixie. You'll like her."

Aaron began jumping on the rocks to make his way around the pond's shore. The sand gave way to mud in some places but it wasn't so soft that he would get stuck. He sank just enough before being able to leap to another spot. He also found banks covered with exposed tree roots. He grabbed at them permitting a better balance on the partly submerged stones.

The whole time he managed to keep his eye on Barry who swam gently over the pond's surface. Ulysses could be seen up in the branches but it was easy to lose sight of him in the leaves because he was so small. The only way Aaron could be certain that it was Ulysses was by his movement.

"I like everyone just fine," Aaron said quietly.

"I'm glad to hear that," Barry said while swimming along in the water. "Everyone here is nice but in their own way. We all depend on the pond and find common ground. It's really to everyone's benefit."

"Why don't Henry and Rex want to go to Good Island?" Aaron asked. He had now found enough dry ground to walk a steady pace.

"It's not for everyone," Barry replied. "Some never make it there. They don't see the point."

"Well, I'm going to make it!" Aaron gleefully shouted.

"Make what?" a duck asked.

"Ah, here she is," Barry said stopping next to a brown feathered duck. "This is Dixie. Meet Aaron!"

"Wow, who is this?" Dixie asked. Her body was covered in brown and black feathers with a stripe of blue that marked her tucked-in wings. Her webbed feet were orange while her beak was yellow. "Do we have a guest? But I've never met him before. Oh dear."

Aaron had now stopped and found some ground to sit on. He leaned back against a rock and breathed deeply to fill his lungs with the fresh air.

"Now Dixie, this is our guest," Barry began. "You don't believe in bad manners, do you?"

"Oh heavens no!" Dixie exclaimed. Aaron flashed a welcoming grin. "I've never held that Dogma. It's just, just... unexpected."

"Dixie has very strict beliefs," Barry began to explain. "Anything new or outside of her beliefs can cause her to, well, appear upset. But appearances are just on the surface, right Aaron?"

"Yes!"

"Well, my Dogma has been with me for as long as I can remember," Dixie demurred. "In fact, I got it from my parents and they got theirs from their parents and so on and so on. If they believed in it and it worked for them, why change? I believe in what I believe and that's that!"

Dixie was picking up sticks with her beak and stacking them in a pile. She waddled over to a bush, lowered her head and picked one up and then waddled back to the pile. She started humming a tune.

"... four, five, six..," Dixie sang.

"Pick-up sticks!" Ulysses chirped.

"Yes!" Dixie responded. "Do you want to play?"

"Of course," Aaron answered. "Do we have enough players?"

"If Ulysses and you play," Dixie said after making her final drop. "We will. Barry, are you interested?"

"I'll pass," Barry answered. Aaron noticed that his body was a deeper shade of gold and wondered if it was because the sun was reflecting off of him.

"Have you ever been to Good Island?" Aaron asked. "I want to go there."

"Heavens no!" Dixie exclaimed. "My parents didn't go there and their parents didn't go there so why should I? It holds no purpose or meaning to me."

"I'll go first," Dixie carefully stuck her beak into the pile and removed a stick. "Now you try."

Aaron picked up a stick and then Ulysses flew down and picked one up with his long black beak. The object of the game was to remove as many sticks without disturbing or moving any other stick. A certain degree of dexterity was required.

"Doesn't seem to be any flowers over here, over here," Ulysses said between turns. "Where are the flowers, Dixie?"

"I have no idea," Dixie replied. "I believe this side of the pond is all flowered out."

Dixie moved her beak in and grabbed a stick. It caused an adjoining one to move and she grumbled because she lost her turn. Aaron was up next and he stuck his hand in carefully and grabbed a stick. He lost his turn too because his stick knocked into another.

The game continued until Ulysses picked up the final stick. Everyone counted what was in front of them. Dixie had eleven, Aaron had nine and Ulysses had thirteen.

Ulysses won!

"Nice job, Ulysses!" Barry chortled from the water. "Way to keep your mind in the game!"

"I believed I was going to win," Dixie protested in disgust by hopping in the water to paddle away. "I was supposed to win. I was supposed to win. I was supposed to...

"Why question anything you were taught?" Dixie asked as she paddled in circles around Barry, leaving a small wake. Ulysses flew to find a flower and Aaron turned to Barry.

"If you believe in something, putting all your hope and trust into it and then it doesn't iron out the way you intended," Aaron asked, "Aren't you setting yourself up to be let down?"

Barry smiled and looked towards Aaron while turning his head to watch an obviously frustrated Dixie.

"You could almost say that a Dogma can weigh you down, making you carry other's thinking with you," Barry continued. "It could make you waddle as you walk."

"Don't worry about her," Barry nodded towards Dixie. "A Dogma can be very constricting and it allows you to either celebrate the world for what it is or criticize it for what it is not. It's like a net that's created to cradle but if you think about it, what's inside you, your intuition, should be your first and only resource. It's all you really need. It's your true Nature."

Aaron looked into the water and saw his reflection next to where Barry was floating. It made him smile.

Chapter 6

The Shedding of the Intellect

"Is this the young man I have been hearing so much about?" a quiet voice slurred.

A garter snake navigated across the ground, its red and black body moving with a serpentine motion until it made its way to an elevated log near the group. Its head was red and neon blue lined its body. The snake's tongue darted quickly in and out of its mouth.

"I was hoping we would see you today," Barry said happily. "Aaron meet Iris, the pond's resident genius."

"He wants to go to Good Island," Dixie began. "It's not a good idea."

"What are the benefits, Aaron?" Iris asked, looking at him directly. "Why go there when everything you need is here?"

"It's just something that I want to do," Aaron explained. "If I can do it, why not?"

"Have you thought about, really applied your Intellect to why it should be considered a good idea?" Iris answered. "Think about it before you do something. There is never any harm in thinking and you might just surprise yourself."

Barry disappeared under the surface of the water before reappearing. He enjoyed the solace and calmness under the water. Aaron noticed that each time he resurfaced his feathers began glowing more. It was as if he was getting brighter.

"Iris is really smart, Aaron," Barry rejoined the conversation. "She can tell you anything about everything. She has an innate ability to acquire knowledge. Ask her anything and she has the answer."

"It's true, you have to believe it," Dixie chortled. "Her Intellect is unmatched!"

"How is it possible to know everything about everything?" Ulysses swooped in and hung stationary over their heads. "I always thought the most you could know is a little about something."

"Like scraping the surface," Barry smiled as his golden body floated gently in the pond's waves. "Iris is undoubtedly smart, no one can argue with that, but an Intellect has a depth which of course means it has its limits and end too. Like a skin, how to measure something that can be shed and replaced...?"

Aaron stared at the water and began removing his shirt and shoes. He had worn his swimming trunks and checked to make sure the waistband strings were tightened in a bow.

With a deep breath, he began wading into the water as everyone watched. He stepped slowly from the shore and the water quickly came to his ankles. He moved further out and it covered his knees. A few more steps and it reached his waist.

"You're doing it!" Ulysses exclaimed. He flew over and hovered over Aaron's head. "You're doing it, Aaron!"

Aaron took a few more steps forward and then stopped. He quickly leapt up on one foot with a startled look on his face.

"What was that!" he yelped. "I just stepped on something!"

"Let me look," Barry said before diving to the bottom. "That was nothing, Aaron. Just a crawfish and they are particularly delicious this time of the year."

Barry was carrying it in his mouth. With a couple of snaps, he swallowed it in one big gulp.

"Delicious indeed!"

"Is that normal?" Aaron asked while regaining his composure. "I've never seen anything like that before."

Barry sighed deeply and looked at Aaron before looking down at the water.

26

"Remember what I told you," Barry said softly. "What I need is not always up here but below. Just because you have not seen it before doesn't mean it doesn't exist."

"Don't fear the unknown?" Aaron asked, looking for approval.

"Exactly, how can you fear what you don't know?" Barry replied. "You are just feeding your fears when they, literally, could be feeding you. It is better to say you know only that you know nothing. Then you remain open to know what you previously did not know."

Aaron laughed at this reflection. He stared down at the water and even though his feet were pressed into the pond's submerged algae and even though he couldn't see them, he began to relax and breathe easier.

"Don't be afraid, Aaron!" Ulysses cheered from above. "Don't be afraid, afraid!"

Aaron picked his feet up and floated on his stomach. He had swam for years and knew he could do this. He looked over at Barry and saw that his body was glowing brighter, like a guide next to him. How he could be afraid when a light would guide him, he thought.

"There you go," Barry encouragingly said. "You're doing it now."

Aaron put his head down and began moving his arms and legs to propel his body. After every other stroke, he turned his head to the side to take another breath. Barry swam alongside and Ulysses followed in the air.

"Remember that there is a flow in the pond," Barry said confidently. "If you can find the flow and stay in it, you will be able to do this with ease."

He had reached the half point between the shore and Good Island. All of a sudden, his leg got twisted in the pond's underwater algae and he stopped.

"What is that?" he said, splashing his hands in the water, trying to tread. "My leg is caught in something."

"Be calm, be calm, Aaron," Ulysses squeaked. "Try to stay still, still."

Barry saw Aaron panic and dove down to where his leg was tangled. He used his beak to cut the weed and watched Aaron's leg relax before diving back towards the surface.

"I don't want to go any further," Aaron gasped between breaths, his hair plastered by the water. "I just don't want to go anymore."

"That's fine," Barry said assuredly. "There's always another day."

Aaron turned to the shore and slowly made his way back. If he could just clear his mind, he could make it.

"You... will... swim, swim...," Ulysses chirped. Aaron only heard a few words in between strokes. "... and … make... Island, Island."

Aaron finally found his footing and slowly walked out of the pond onto its shore.

"I thought I could make it," he muttered to himself.

"You will," Barry encouragingly said.

Aaron looked over and Barry was smiling at him. He began to put on his shirt and shoes. He tied the laces and gave out a sigh before looking out at the island. The momentary defeat was washed away by Barry's optimism.

Tomorrow is another chance, he thought to himself. After saying goodbye he retraced his steps back through the forest. The whole way back he thought about swimming to the island without fear. He knew he could do it.

Chapter 7

A Sluggish Perception

It was raining the next day but Aaron still found his way to the pond. Navigating the forest was a cinch and this time he saw earthworms crawling through the soft mud.

As he got closer to the pond, Aaron heard a wail echo across the water. The deep, low call sliced through the natural forest noises to form a natural symphony.

Aaron got to the shore and looked for Barry. He was nowhere to be found! Aaron looked down the shore to where they were the day before. Nothing. He looked the other way. Nothing. Is he behind the island where I can't see him, he wondered. Another wail rang out, echoing across the air.

"What are you doing?" a voice suddenly called out.

Aaron looked around and saw a snail.

"I'm trying to find my friend, Barry," Aaron strained his neck to look further down the shore. "Do you know him?"

"Know him, yes," the snail sputtered the words out slowly. Her shell was brown and had a circular curvature. Her body was soft and gelatinous with two stems extending upward from the side of her head. "He is one of a kind."

"Hey, what do you think of this rain, this rain?" Ulysses swooped in. "Oh hey, you've met Patty. Anyone know where Barry is, Barry is?"

"I'd say he's over there," Patty quietly answered. "But it's all what you think."

"What do you mean?" Aaron asked.

"It's all based on your Perception," she replied. "Everything you know, think or imagine is based on what you can see, hear, taste, smell, and touch. It's common sense.

"For instance, I can only see things in black and white," Patty continued. "Is that how the world really is or are there other colors? I cannot see them so they really aren't necessary for me."

"So you can't tell that the sky is blue?" Aaron asked.

"What is blue?" Patty retorted. "It means nothing to me."

"I'll do a quick search, quick search for Barry." Ulysses' wings beat the air rapidly and he zipped around the edge of the pond. He flew out over the water and then back to a branch. After a while, Aaron couldn't see him anymore and so he looked back at Patty.

"Did you hear Barry's call?" Aaron asked.

"Oh yes, he often does that when he's happy," Patty replied. "Or when he's trying to find someone."

"I like his voice, it sounds very... soulful," Aaron said. "It's very deep and seems to be calling out to something...."

"Or someone," Patty interrupted.

"Who then?" Aaron asked.

"Only Barry knows," she replied quietly.

"Have you ever been to Good Island?" Aaron asked.

"I don't really get around a lot," Patty said softly. "I have no need or purpose for going there."

Aaron looked up and saw Barry swimming towards him. Ulysses was hovering overhead and keeping pace with him. The pond's surface was showing divots from the pelting raindrops.

"I wasn't sure if you were coming today since it was raining," Barry said when he was close enough for Aaron to hear. "Ulysses told me you were here."

"How could I not?" Aaron responded excitedly. "I love coming here."

Barry smiled and his coat of golden feathers were glowing brighter than yesterday. Was it the rain, Aaron wondered.

"I'm glad you met Patty," Barry replied. "She often comes out in the rain."

"I come out when I think it is right," Patty said. "Everything is based on Perception. There is no other way around it."

"Could you explain, explain?" Ulysses squeaked.

"Sure, it's easy," she began. "You're a hummingbird and I'm a snail and so our Perceptions are different. You like flowers for food and I like flowers for beauty. Perception is everything, just as it is how you look at something."

"Can they be changed?" Aaron asked.

"Perceptions, yes, but it is very difficult," Patty said quietly. "Once set, they rarely change. Why would they? They've served their purpose so why question their utility?"

"What about a deeper and more meaningful perspective?" Barry suggested. "What if a greater awareness was possible, wouldn't that be worthy of pursuing?"

"I don't understand....," Patty whispered.

"Our true Nature, Patty," Barry continued. "Every sense is identified but the most important one is forgotten. Our Perception is misaligned because we use all the common senses except the most important one of all. It's our connection to each other and all of Nature."

Patty stared at Barry and didn't answer.

"So you're saying that you control your own Perception," Aaron intervened. "Really everything is either an obstacle or opportunity and you're the one that decides, right? It's just how you look at it?"

"Right!" Barry said. "If you taste something, say Brussels sprouts, they can be either bitter or sweet, but it is up to you to decide. So much in life is like that."

Barry looked at Aaron with an approving smile. Ulysses looked down from a tree branch and nodded his head too.

Chapter 8

Cracking the Nut of Time

A branch rustled and Turner bounded out of the forest. Covered in brown fur, the squirrel had small pointy ears with whiskers sprouting from his cheeks. He stood up on his hind feet and revealed a stomach covered in a white coat of fur.

"Anybody got the Time?" Turner asked. "I can't tell what Time it is."

"Ah, Turner," Barry responded with a chuckle. "Always concerned about Time. No, I don't know what Time it is. It's nothing I ever worry about."

"Worry about!" Turner exclaimed. "Worry about! There's never enough Time. How do you measure anything without Time? I don't understand!"

"Look at it this way...," Barry began to respond.

"If we don't have Time," Turner interrupted. "How do we know when to do something? Schedule something? Plan something?"

"The sun comes up and then the moon comes up," Barry continued calmly. "Light or dark, it's still the same day and that is more than enough to get done what needs to be done."

"I'll never understand!" Turner screeched. "There's never enough Time to get everything done. Always busy, busy, busy! Never enough Time!"

Turner darted back into the forest and the leaves of the bushes rustled. He reemerged with nuts stuffed in his cheek. He tried to walk while holding a stack in his paws but tripped and scattered them.

"Poor Turner, always so worried, so worried," Ulysses chirped.

"The past is a memory, the future is just expectation, and all we have and will ever have is now," Barry said to Aaron. "So much in the world is assigned value by others. Concepts that are really illusory are nothing more than a divergence from your eternal true Nature."

"But the sun and moon rise and fall in the sky," Aaron countered. "Isn't that a sign of Time?"

"It is the same, day and night," Barry answered quickly. "Sweet, bitter, light, dark, it is all the same. Time was created by us to measure and identify something that is and will always exist."

"It's your goal to get to Good Island, right?" Barry asked.

"Of course."

"Well, the Time will come where you will make an effort to get there," Barry continued. "That is the value you place on that Time, to reach that place. You will do it when the Time is right for you. Time is simply measured by movement."

Aaron noticed that the rain was letting up and the clouds were beginning to part and lighten. *I knew it would stop*, he thought.

"Want to try to swim to Good Island again, Aaron?" Barry asked. Ulysses perched on a branch above them, waiting for an answer.

"Yes, today is the day and now is a good Time," Aaron said. "How's the water?"

"Like everything, you get used to it once you're in," Barry replied. "Hot or cold, it always remains the same."

Chapter 9

The Flight of the Ego

"What do we have here!" a deep voice bellowed. A big white stork floated across the sky, casting a shadow on the pond before landing near the group. "Is this the Aaron everyone keeps mentioning? I just had to meet him!"

"What brings you to our shores, Edison?" Patty asked.

"I'm the tallest and the best so why shouldn't I stop by?" Edison boasted. "Shouldn't Aaron have the chance to meet the greatest on the pond? Har, har, har!"

"Such an Ego, Ego," Ulysses squeaked before zipping to another branch for a better view. "Never afraid of showing his Ego."

"Why shouldn't I?" Edison smirked. "If you're the best, shouldn't you show it to others? Prove yourself always. It teaches others who the best is and I am the best!"

"Your Ego defines you, drives you, and determines who you are," Edison said sternly. "By all measures, it is the best measurement of you. Everyone, big or small, has one and your success and failure depends on how well you develop and feed it. It's what drives your survival skills."

"Can it create beauty?" Barry chimed in. "Or justice and harmony?"

"What?" Edison asked in surprise.

"Can it give you happiness?" Barry continued. "Is it not just a fire inside that has an insatiable hunger to consume, with no limits or boundaries? If left unchecked won't it consume you from within? An Ego can soar but is really just an extension, like our wings."

"But it has served me so well," Edison boomed. "Look at my beautiful feathers, my strong legs and powerful beak. I am clearly the best here!"

39

"See Aaron, here is another example of allowing another quality to cloud your true Nature," Barry said, motioning to him with his wing. "Why create an obstacle that clouds your connection to the universal Nature? Matching your nature with Nature is the true source of happiness."

"Have you been to Good Island?" Aaron asked.

"Har, har, har, that tiny piece of land is too small for me!" Edison squawked mockingly. "Why settle for a little when I can have a lot! I need more, more, more and claim everything I set my eyes on!"

"A little bird told me that you can see better from it," Aaron replied.

The sun was now completely out and the air became warmer. Aaron looked and saw the forest appear greener and the wet sand on the shore was turning from dark brown to grey. The water was also turning bluer, reflecting the sky above. A few white clouds marked it but other than that, it was blue as far as the eye could see.

The rain had made the pond and forest appear new.

Rex and Iris reappeared on the pond's shore with Turner. Dixie paddled over from a marshy bank of grass and Henry jumped on a beached log.

Chapter 10

Standing on Good Island

"Well Aaron, are you ready?" Barry glowed. His body was lighting the water around him now, serving as a golden beacon.

"Yes," he replied, removing his poncho, shirt and shoes. His tugged his pants off to reveal his bathing trunks underneath. He pulled the strings tighter and retied the bow on his trunks. "I'm ready to go to Good Island."

"You have no Reason to go!" Rex cried. "Don't be so hasty about it!"

"You've never had a Habit of going, so why start now?" Henry questioned. "Stay true to yourself and you'll never have to venture out!"

"Whose Dogma is weighing you down?" Dixie cried. "No one here, I assure you! Readjust your beliefs to mine. Please listen!"

"Use your Intellect and think about it," Iris chastised. "What in the world could be there to justify going?"

"Your Perception is wrong and not serving you," Patty announced slowly. "Change your course now- don't change the way you perceive the world."

"You'll never have enough Time!" Turner screeched. "There's only so much Time. Don't waste it!"

"Even if you make it, your Ego will never be as big as mine!" Edison cackled. "What are you trying to prove? Inflating your Ego will never get you to Good Island!"

"Don't listen to them, to them," Ulysses chirped reassuredly. He was hovering over Aaron's head. "You can do this, do this."

"I know I can," Aaron said as he walked to the pond's edge. As he did the day before, he waded into the water. At first it felt colder but then he adjusted and it felt natural. *Why should I listen to those who have never been to Good Island? Only Barry and Ulysses have been there and they're with me on this.*

Aaron began floating in the water till his body was parallel with the surface. He took a deep breath and lowered his face. He began moving his legs and arms to propel himself through the water like he had done so many times before. Barry paddled next to him, making the pond appear brilliantly golden, and Aaron could see Ulysses hovering over him from the corner of his eye.

He got to the midpoint he was at yesterday and smiled as his feet touched the pond's submerged algae. *You won't trip me up this time*, he thought.

He stopped and began treading water to look back at the shore. Reason, Habit, Dogma, Intellect, Perception, Time, and Ego were left on the shore and were nowhere close to him. He had left them all and now all that was left was him. He had to rely on what he had, his innate strength to animate and propel him to Good Island. He would make it because it was his destination.

Barry was beginning to glow brighter and brighter as they got closer to Good Island. Aaron could see him clearly now through the water even as he was swimming.

The water was beginning to get shallow and Aaron lifted his head. Good Island was just a few feet in front of him. The pond's mushy bottom became sandy and he could stand up. He began to wade closer, his legs moving steadily through the water. He put his hand on a large boulder jutting out of the water and hoisted himself up on it.

Water streamed off Aaron as he managed to keep his balance hopping across the boulders to the beach. He felt anew. Barry stayed in the water and Ulysses fluttered overhead. Barry let out a deep low soulful wail that echoed across the entire pond and surrounding forest.

"Who were you calling to all those times?" Aaron asked as he rubbed the water out of his eyes. He shook his head for a few seconds to dry his hair.

"I've been calling to you," Barry answered quietly. "A soul always calls out and is heard by anyone willing to listen. The more you listened, the stronger and brighter I became, thus easier to guide you."

Aaron looked out across the pond from Good Island and he could see for the first time what he had been missing. The entire forest was illuminated and brought into focus and he could see, really see for the first time. The Whole picture. Aaron now understood why he was there and he was happy.

He was happy.

www.ingramcontent.com/pod-product-compliance
Lightning Source LLC
Chambersburg PA
CBHW080552030426
42337CB00024B/4850